Original title:
Space Dust Diaries

Copyright © 2025 Creative Arts Management OÜ
All rights reserved.

Author: Seraphina Caldwell
ISBN HARDBACK: 978-1-80567-768-0
ISBN PAPERBACK: 978-1-80567-889-2

# Fragments of Light: The Journey of a Wanderer

In a ship made of jelly beans,
I sail on marshmallow streams.
With gummy bears as my crew,
We giggle at starlit views.

Wormholes are just silly bends,
Where time and space seem to be friends.
I floated by a comet's tail,
And traded snacks in a cosmic gale.

The Milky Way's a chocolate bar,
Each bite takes me near and far.
I might just get lost in a snack,
As stars wink from the galaxy's back.

## Celestial Ink and Stardust Traces

I found a pen made of light,
To write my tales in the night.
With ink that shimmers and glows,
I penned the tales of cosmic shows.

Galaxies play hide and seek,
As I scribble each twinkling peak.
Planets dancing in a line,
I giggle, saying, 'That's divine!'

Asteroids with silly faces,
Crashing into starry places.
They say, 'Hey, don't take a chance!'
I just smile and join their dance.

## Enigmas of the Expanding Universe

Why do stars wear silly hats?
Or float around like friendly cats?
I asked a quasar, 'What's the deal?'
It winked and said, 'Just how I feel!'

Black holes just love to consume,
Swallowing light like a vacuum.
I tried to jump in for some fun,
But ended up doing a cosmic run.

Each nebula with colors bright,
Looks like candy in broad daylight.
I twirled and laughed in sheer delight,
Chasing comets flying by at night.

## Luminescent Tales from the Cosmic Sea

In oceans of light, I take a dip,
With jellyfish that like to flip.
Stars swim by in disco balls,
Echoing laughter as music calls.

The moon played chess with a sunbeam,
I joined in with a silly dream.
"Checkmate!" the sun did cheer and shout,
While I just floated about, no doubt.

I built a sandcastle of light,
With aliens dancing in sheer delight.
As waves of stardust wash ashore,
I laugh and play forevermore.

## The Galaxy's Letters

In a box of stars, I found a note,
Written by a comet, it made me gloat.
It said, "Dear Earth, I love your blue,
But your traffic jams? Who knew?"

With ink made of stardust, it drew a laugh,
Jupiter replied with a giant giraffe.
"Come take a ride on my swirling rings,
But first, let's dance—see what joy it brings!"

## Fragments of Light

A flicker in the sky, a cheeky wink,
From a star too bright, don't make me think.
"I'm not showing off!" it seemed to say,
"Just practicing my moves for the Milky Way!"

The Moon rolled its eyes, looking quite cool,
"Under your glow, I still feel a fool.
But let's have a party, a cosmic affair,
Where meteors drop in with multicolor flare!"

## Orbits of Longing

A planet named Bob sings soft, silly tunes,
While flirting with Venus under bright maroon moons.
"Do you like dance?" he jovially asks,
Shy planets blush, dropping their masked tasks.

In the asteroid belt, they spin and sway,
Practicing their moves, come what may.
But Bob trips over, oh what a sight!
He dances alone through the velvet night!"

## Starry-Eyed Confessions

Two stars in the night shared secrets quite bold,
One has a crush on a black hole so old.
"He pulls me in close, it's thrilling, you see!"
The other replies, "That's not love, it's a spree!"

They giggle and twinkle, their laughter so bright,
For cosmos can weave tales both wrong and right.
"Remember the sun? He's still shining like mad,
But with all those flares, he's just a bit bad!"

## **Fragments of the Cosmos**

Once a comet lost its way,
It thought a black hole was a cafe.
With a sprinkle of stars on its tail,
It ordered a drink, then started to sail.

Galaxies giggled at its plight,
While nebulae blushed, oh what a sight!
The universe chuckled, caught in a whirl,
As stardust danced, in a comical swirl.

## Stardust Sentiments

A meteorite wrote a love note,
To a planet that just couldn't float.
It said, 'You're spherical, I like your vibe,'
But the planet just rolled, too shy to subscribe.

Asteroids laughed as they tumbled by,
'What a rom-com!' they'd giggle and sigh.
While cosmic rays made silly jokes,
'This love story is just for folks!'

**Echoes of the Universe**

A black hole whispered secrets so deep,
But the stars just snickered, could hardly keep.
'What's with the gravity? You're such a bore!'
They twinkled and teased, wanting more.

The cosmos echoed tales of delight,
Of a supernova that danced every night.
With a bang and a flash, it stole the show,
While planets rolled their eyes, and said, 'Oh no!'

## Galactic Remnants

In a far-away corner, old dust bunnies play,
Tossing old starlight in a quirky ballet.
While satellites snickered from up high,
'What a mess! They'll float 'til they fly!'

Comets stashed snacks in time's cosmic pack,
'Hey, want a donut? I've got a whole stack!'
And black holes just spun, full of disdain,
Saying, 'You're all weird, but we love the game!'

## Tales from the Infinite

In the void where lost socks hide,
Galactic giggles collide.
Planets toss their dust like fries,
While comets wink from distant skies.

Aliens dance on Saturn's rings,
Trading tales and silly things.
A black hole swallows all the cheer,
Leaving just the laughter here.

Stars debate who shines the most,
While asteroids plan a wild roast.
Gravity keeps them all in line,
But space is where the jokes align.

So lift your glass of cosmic pop,
And never let your spirits drop.
For up above the Earth so bright,
The universe is one big night!

## Starwoven Stories

Bouncing stars with silly names,
Like Twinkletoes that play their games.
Galaxies play hide and seek,
While supernovas giggle and squeak.

Meteor showers rain down laughs,
As stardust weaves the finest gaffes.
Each twinkle tells a tale so bold,
Of cosmic pranks from days of old.

Black holes swirl in secret fun,
Sucking in the rays of sun.
Tangled tales that twist and turn,
In the sky where bright stars burn.

So grab a seat in the glowing sky,
Let laughter echo, never shy.
In the vast and wondrous play,
Cosmic joy is here to stay!

## Luminous Memories

Once in a galaxy far away,
Naptime was a starry play.
Little comets with bedtime dreams,
Floating on milk and cosmic creams.

Galaxies had bedtime stories,
Filled with goofy starry glories.
Planets giggled with delight,
As meteors danced through the night.

In the glow of twinkling light,
Asteroids battled in playful fight.
Oh, the laughter that would rise,
As starlit wonders painted skies.

So cherish every cosmic beam,
For laughter fuels the universe's dream.
With memories woven bright and fine,
In the glow of a starlit line!

## Cosmic Echoes

In the whispers of the cosmic breeze,
Stars play hide-and-seek with ease.
A giggly moon with a cheeky grin,
Sends echoes swirling like a spin.

The universe tells funny tales,
Of sneaky suns and comet trails.
Space is filled with witty charms,
As laughter dances in its arms.

Planets form a jolly band,
Strumming tunes with stardust hand.
Satellites hum a merry tune,
Under the light of a winking moon.

So let the echoes of joy resound,
In every corner of space unbound.
For in this vast and funny show,
Laughter is the star we blow!

## Constellation Whispers

Stars gossip in the night,
Twinkling secrets take flight.
Planets laugh and play around,
Floating jokes so profound.

A comet zooms, a mischievous grin,
'Catch me if you can, I'm the fastest spin!'
Meteor showers rain on down,
Like starry confetti from a cosmic clown.

Asteroids trade their silly tales,
Dodging satellites, they leave trails.
Galaxies shake with laughter's tune,
Under the watchful gaze of the moon.

In the universe, we all share a jest,
A cosmic punchline, who's the best?
With each twinkle and every flight,
The cosmos dances, oh, what a sight!

## Galactic Echoes

In an echo of space, I hear a laugh,
A distant nebula sharing a gaffe.
Supernovae burst with glee,
'Look at me, I'm a star, can't you see?'

Black holes spin tales of endless fright,
'Come closer, let's have a dance tonight!'
Quasars flicker, a cosmic show,
While aliens giggle, just below.

Planets waltz in a graceful line,
Orbs of wonder, spinning divine.
Every echo holds a pun so wise,
In the vastness, humor never dies.

Warping time with a twist of fate,
The universe knows how to create.
So strap in tight and take a ride,
Through cosmic jokes on a comet's slide!

## A Moment in the Expanse

Floating through the stellar pond,
Space turtles drift, so fond.
With tiny hats and ice-cream cones,
They munch through time on rubbery bones.

A sunbeam sits, sipping its tea,
While green moons dance in cosmic glee.
Count the stars, can't take it slow,
They're juggling planets in a cosmic show.

Galactic squirrels scamper about,
Collecting stardust for a grand night out.
With every leap, a flux of cheer,
In this vast expanse, fun is near.

So let's embrace the odd and bizarre,
In a universe that's never ajar.
For every moment is a thrill,
In the cosmic carnival, we find our fill!

## Astrology of Memory

Stars align with a giggly twist,
Reminding us of moments missed.
Retrograde brings a laugh or two,
'You thought you'd call? Guess we'll skip that stew!'

The moon chuckles, oh so bright,
'Lost your keys? Just check the light!'
Comets zoom, with tales of yore,
Each memory a cosmic encore.

Zodiac signs are in the fray,
Taurus tripping over his own ballet.
While Libras weigh each punchline right,
Creating humor that sparks delight.

So consult the stars for laughter's spark,
In the vast cosmos, we leave our mark.
With each celestial flicker and play,
Memories glitter as we dance away!

## Wanderlust of the Stellar Nomads

In a rocket ship made of cheese,
We zoom past Jupiter with ease.
Mars is pink, or maybe red,
We'll take a nap in a crater bed.

Alien tourists taking a snap,
One said, 'Where's the cosmic map?'
They clutched their phones, oh what a sight,
Snapping selfies in the starlight!

On Saturn's rings, we built a slide,
With moonbeams as our joyful ride.
We giggled as we floated high,
Laughing together, oh my, oh my!

Galactic food trucks all around,
Delivering ice cream, free and round.
We taste meteoroid fudge delight,
Blasting off 'til the morning light!

## A Tapestry of Light in the Cosmic Loom

Stars woven with laughter and cheer,
Creating patterns far and near.
Comets tailing glittery trails,
As we tell whimsical tales!

Nebulae dance in shades of pink,
They swirl around like a cosmic drink.
'Extra whipped cream,' we always plea,
'And don't forget the galaxy!'

Supernovas burst, oh what a show,
Scattering confetti, watch it go!
Planets spin in a conga line,
Our party's the best in space divine!

Cosmic yarn, we knit with glee,
Making scarves of infinity.
We wear them proudly, twirl and play,
In our quasar masquerade today!

## Stardust Trails: The Path to the Unknown

With telescopes built from old soda cans,
We stargaze while munching on space fries and plans.
Each twinkle a rumor, a story anew,
We chart the unknown in our colorful view.

A black hole's a party, a swirling delight,
Where time plays tricks, and the snacks are just right.
We've lost a few socks, they danced out of sight,
Caught in the fabric of cosmic kite flight!

Asteroids singing their rocky old songs,
And Martians teach us the latest wrongs.
Chasing meteors, we run with a shout,
In the stardust trails, no fear, no doubts!

Exploring the cosmos, we search high and low,
For ice cream planets and rainbows that glow.
Each puff of the Milky Way's frosty mist,
Brings laughter and joy that can't be dismissed!

# Radiance of the Cosmic Landscape

In the cosmic park where all stargazers roam,
Alien dogs bark from their planet's foam.
Every swing's a comet, each slide a bright star,
Together we reach for whatever we are!

The sun, wearing shades, shows off its flare,
While moons play hide and seek in midair.
Galactic giggles echo out wide,
As we surf the cosmic ocean, a joyride!

Astro-butterflies flutter by with flair,
Painting the dark with colors that compare.
We dance 'neath the shimmering starlit guise,
In the cosmic carnival, we rise and rise!

And the milky streams keep flowing by,
As laughter echoes beneath the sky.
Oh what a journey, oh what a ride,
In this radiant landscape, we'll always reside!

## Echoes of the Universe in Silken Nights

A comet sneezed, it whizzed right by,
Leaving stardust sniffling in the sky.
Planets giggle in their cosmic chase,
Spinning tales of interstellar grace.

The moon once tripped, and what a sight,
Tumbled through asteroids, oh what a flight!
Galaxies swirl in a merry dance,
Winking at stars, they take their chance.

Black holes burp with a slurpy sound,
Swallowing light, spinning it 'round.
Saturn's rings sparkle, oh what a tease,
Tickling Jupiter's storms with ease.

Each twinkling star has a secret scheme,
Plotting mischief in the cosmic dream.
Echoes of laughter fill the night air,
In this vast dark, there's magic to share.

## Nebula's Lament: A Star's Farewell

Once a star with a glorious flare,
Now it flickers, a celestial dare.
A nebula sighed, shedding its light,
Saying goodbye, oh what a fright.

With cosmic confetti, they bid adieu,
Stars threw a party, a lively crew.
Things got wild; they danced on a whim,
Until a black hole swallowed them in.

"Don't worry," whispered a wise old quasar,
"More will be born, just look from afar!"
Supernovae giggled, explosions galore,
Filling the cosmos with glittery lore.

So here's to the stars, both near and far,
Each one a tale in this dark bazaar.
With laughter and love, they light up the abyss,
Even in departures, they share cosmic bliss.

## Astral Memoirs from the Edge of Infinity

In a distant realm where space-time bends,
Planets write letters to cosmic friends.
A supernova once penned with flair,
"I exploded! You should have been there!"

Neutron stars play chess with a twist,
Giggling at meteors they can't resist.
Black holes compete for the loudest roar,
While quasars send gigabytes to shore.

Shooting stars wish to be comets for days,
Fumbling through dust in a playful haze.
Galactic gossip flies through the void,
With each spark of laughter, worlds are buoyed.

In the silken dark, they share their dreams,
Expanding possibilities, or so it seems.
So grab your telescope, come take a peek,
At the funny side of the cosmic mystique.

# Constellation Confessions Beneath the Milky Way

Beneath the blanket of the night sky,
Constellations chatter, oh me, oh my!
Orion winks at a shy little star,
Saying, "Join the fun, you're never too far!"

Cassiopeia brags of her sparkly crown,
While Draco hisses, "Please put it down!"
The Great Bear giggles, a sight to see,
Rolling in stardust, wild and free.

Each shooting star carries silly wishes,
For interstellar hugs and cosmic kisses.
They dance through the void, shared laughter and cheer,
In the stillness of night, they create their sphere.

So raise your eyes to this dazzling display,
Join in the laughter, let worries drift away.
For in the cosmos, we're all tied together,
Sharing secrets and joy, now and forever.

## Cosmic Dreams

In a rocket made of cheese,
I zoom past stars with ease,
The Milky Way calls me sweet,
With chocolate comets for a treat.

Galactic cows go moo at night,
They dance with planets, what a sight!
Jupiter throws a birthday bash,
While Saturn's rings go twinkle-flash.

I wear my helmet made of foam,
While moon pies feel like home,
Nebulas wear fluffy hats,
As space critters chat with bats.

When I land on Mars to play,
I jump around and shout hooray!
With aliens sharing silly jokes,
We laugh till we can't breathe, those folks!

## Echoes Beyond the Stars

The stars laugh as they twinkle bright,
Telling tales of their cosmic flight,
A vacuum cleaner spins around,
Sucking up space dust from the ground.

A comet trips and takes a fall,
Bumping into the moon's big ball,
They giggle, making quite a mess,
A stardust party, we must confess.

Planets play a game of tag,
While Saturn gives a friendly wag,
Mars throws confetti from its craters,
Making fun of the slow-paced waiters.

Echoes of laughter fill the air,
Cosmic chuckles everywhere,
In this universe full of glee,
We dance while sipping space-time tea!

## Celestial Fantasies

A star and a planet went for tea,
They argued over who's the most free,
With cosmic cookies piled on hand,
They planned a road trip to dreamland.

Asteroids join in the fun-filled ride,
Hitching a lift, they're full of pride,
Through constellations, they zoom and whirl,
With giggles echoing around the swirl.

The sun wears shades, looking so cool,
As they play hopscotch on a cosmic pool,
Galaxies twirl in a whimsical dance,
While black holes spin, given half a chance.

In this realm of celestial play,
Stardust wonder leads the way,
Where laughter lights the darkened sky,
And dreams of space never say goodbye!

## **Whims of the Universe**

The universe throws a giant fair,
With stars in hats and cosmic hair,
Pluto juggles asteroids with flair,
While meteors dance without a care.

Saturn spins like a dizzy top,
With all its friends, they never stop,
They paint the night with silly hues,
While comets play hopscotch in their shoes.

An alien chef serves soup of light,
With flavors that tickle and excite,
They serve it up on silver plates,
While bright satellites hope for dates.

Who knew that in the void so vast,
Cosmic pranks and giggles would last?
In the whims of the universe we find,
That laughter transcends all of time blind!

## Twilight Dreams

In the twilight, dreams take flight,
Shooting stars and space squirrels bite.
Galaxies dance, with a comical flair,
Aliens snicker, with purple hair.

Cosmic hiccups from the nearby moon,
While asteroids hum a silly tune.
Floating cows and cats so spry,
In zero gravity, they leap and fly.

Wormholes giggle, a portal's tease,
Time feels silly, like jello breeze.
Planets trip, on their cosmic jig,
A dance-off with a friendly sprig.

Bouncing bubbles of galactic goo,
Laughing at comets zooming through.
Twilight hugs with a goofy grin,
In this dream, let the fun begin!

## Resonance of the Cosmic

In the cosmic hum, a bubble pops,
Galactic giggles, and laughter flops.
Stars twinkle in a cheeky way,
Winking at night like they're on play.

Black holes chuckle, 'Come take a ride!'
With gravity games, they swing and slide.
Silly satellites spin in a whirl,
Dancing around a rocky pearl.

Meteor showers rain sprinkles of fun,
As cosmic crickets chirp one by one.
Nebulas puff like a giant cloud,
Joking with stardust, all laughing loud.

Auroras twist in brilliant hue,
As planets tease in a playful crew.
And every light-year feels like a joke,
In the resonance where stardust spoke!

# Remnants of Light

Remnants of light, a shining spree,
Glowing space critters sip their tea.
Galaxies chuckle, "Did you see that?"
A moon with glasses, now that's a fact!

Whirling around in a cosmic race,
Cumulus clouds with a smiley face.
Asteroids wearing hats so bright,
Slide past comets in a playful fright.

Time zippers and wormholes weave,
Telling tales that we can't believe.
Laughter echoes through the stars,
As planets drum on their candy bars.

Jokes of black holes, how they devour,
Even light's scared in this odd hour.
But in this chaos, we find delight,
In the sweet remnants of cosmic light.

## Stardust Journeys

Stardust journeys on a bumpy ride,
With comets giggling, side by side.
Riding waves of the cosmic sea,
Space travelers shout, "Whee! Look at me!"

Galactic maps with crayons drawn,
Lead to a land of the whimsical dawn.
Planets teasing in their lovely coats,
Shuffle in rhythm to the cosmic notes.

Floating fish with their fins of glow,
Dancing around in a twinkling show.
They wink at the stars with an inside joke,
While spacetime pirouettes in a smoky cloak.

Jump aboard the starlit train,
Where the universe plays a silly game.
Each journey's end is just the start,
Of laughter and joy—space, a big heart!

## Tales of the Unknown

In the dark where the odd things roam,
A sock reported lost from home.
It danced with glee in starlit air,
While gazing down on a cosmic fair.

A comet sneezed, what a sight!
It scattered sparkles, pure delight.
A rubber duck just floated by,
Sipping on tea and pie in the sky.

Peeking through a cosmic door,
Aliens play hopscotch on the floor.
With galactic giggles, they take their chance,
Inviting us all to join the dance.

So if you hear laughter from above,
Just know it's space having fun, with love.
Amidst the stars, there's always a clue,
Life's silly moments for me and you.

## Astral Diaries

In my journal of stars, I write each night,
About UFOs that shine so bright.
Last Tuesday's food fight wasn't a hoax,
Martian spaghetti covered in folks.

I scribble tales of a two-headed cat,
Who juggles black holes, imagine that!
It barks at comets with quite the flair,
A cosmic pet with spacey hair.

Whispers of moons that love to sing,
They harmonize while fridge magnets cling.
In zero-gravity, they sway along,
Creating a chorus, a silly song.

Oh, the mishaps in celestial prose,
Like planets wearing mismatched clothes.
A dance party with stars, oh what a riot,
In the grand universe, you find the quiet!

## Celestial Horizons

Up in the cosmos, what do I see?
A satellite sipping on cosmic tea.
With biscuits made of light and dust,
He winks at a meteor, oh what a must!

Galaxies giggle and twirl with glee,
As they spin tales of gravity-free.
Stars toss confetti from high above,
Celebrating space in a party of love.

An asteroid cruising on a skateboard,
Racing around the moons, never bored.
Planetary races with no finish line,
Where every blunder is simply divine.

So here's to the wonders that drift through air,
Full of quirks that we seldom share.
In the vastness of sky, both silly and bright,
We laugh with the cosmos, what a delight!

## Chronicles of the Celestial

In a galaxy far, far away,
An alien danced in a bright array,
He tripped on a comet's tail,
And shouted, 'Well, that's a fail!'

His buddy, a star, gave a wink,
'You should try not to think!
Floating here is quite sublime,
Just don't step on the space-time!'

A black hole laughed with a swirl,
'You boys are in quite a whirl!
Keep your feet off my event horizon,
Or I just might send you flying!'

They laughed as the planets twirled,
Gravity? How absurd, this world!
So they skated on rings of Saturn,
While the universe just did pattern.

## Stardust Reflections

On a meteorite, two cats sat,
Purring and plotting where they're at,
One said, 'Is this a shooting star?
Or just our dreams gone too far?'

A rocket flew by, much to their shock,
'Hey, can we hitch a ride, or just walk?'
The pilot blinked, with a frown,
'No cats allowed in my shiny town!'

They licked their paws, quite dismayed,
'Let's sneak in, we'll be well-played!
With soft fur and mischief keen,
Cosmic travelers, yet to be seen!'

But as they plotted, a hiccup arose,
They bumbled and tumbled - oh no, oh no!
Into the void, off they went,
Two foolish cats on a grand event!

## Lunar Letters

A space snail wrote a letter today,
To his friend, who lives far away,
'With the moon cheese I've got,
You'd love it, I swear, it's quite hot!'

He sealed it tight with a cosmic glue,
But forgot, the stars he flew through,
Brought it back with a twisty swirl,
'Careful now, don't cause a whirl!'

His friend replied, in a fractal rhyme,
'Thanks for the snail mail, I'll make time!
But please don't send it via bright rays,
Last time, it got lost in a maze!'

So they laughed under the glittering night,
Crafting tales of their silly flight,
In the lunar glow, friendship grew,
Even when letters stuck like glue!

## Meteoric Reflections

Two meteors raced in a cosmic chase,
One said, 'I'm winning! Keep up the pace!'
But one had a plan, oh so sly,
   'Watch me as I take to the sky!'

They zoomed past planets, dodged a sun,
   'Hey wait! This isn't quite fun!
I didn't sign up for solar flares,
Or dodging the moon's snarky glares!'

With a sudden turn, one flipped quite bold,
   'Let's make this an interstellar fold!'
They spiraled and swirled in the dark,
Laughing, they set off a cosmic spark!

But as they giggled, they started to slow,
'Uh-oh, what's this? We're lost, you know!'
The galaxies winked at their silly race,
Two meteors stopped, finding their place.

## Transient Gazes Through the Astral Veil

In pajamas, I float on a comet,
With a snack in hand, what a profit!
Stars do a jig, they know how to party,
As I dance with them, feeling all hearty.

Aliens laugh at my shimmery moves,
I stumble and trip, but what's there to prove?
They raise their antennas, trying to cheer,
While I giggle and tumble, with no hint of fear.

Galactic grapes are my favorite treat,
I munch and I crunch to an extraterrestrial beat.
Orbiting planets, with a wink and a grin,
Who knew the cosmos had such a spin?

In this astral bazaar, I'm the silliest sight,
Juggling asteroids late into the night.
With laughter as light as a nebula's dream,
I wave to the stars, bursting with gleam.

## The Poetic Voyage of Cosmic Shores.

On a surfboard, I ride solar flares,
Dodging space turtles with brightly colored wares.
Galaxies swirl like cotton candy dreams,
As I giggle and glide on these gleaming beams.

Sand made of stardust, so soft on my toes,
I build quirky castles, as a comical prose.
Starfish are dancing; they're doing the twist,
While I take selfies with a galactic mist.

The moon serves ice cream, with sprinkles of light,
I lick the void, oh, what a delight!
Neon comets race in a lighthearted chase,
And I laugh so hard, I float off in space.

Time runs in circles, it sways and it bends,
With friends who are planets and mischievous ends.
We toast with moonbeams, in cosmic elation,
This fun-filled voyage needs a celebration!

**Stardust Chronicles**

In my rocket, I keep a diary of laughs,
Drawing doodles of black holes and silly graphs.
Meteor showers shower me with spritz,
As I scribble my dreams with the starry kits.

Cosmic cookies are baked in a sun's warm glow,
Each bite's a giggle—a sweet afterglow.
The Milky Way winks with its creamy delight,
As I dance with the comets, oh, what a sight!

I pen down the tales of quirky space friends,
Like squishy-eyed aliens with gumball amends.
Each chapter's a riot, a hilarious play,
In this stardust world where we frolic and sway.

With laughter as fuel, we ride through the night,
Painting the cosmos with joy and delight.
In this funny realm of cosmic remark,
Every single page sparks a whimsical spark.

## **Celestial Whispers**

Whispers of laughter float through the black,
Planets exchange gossip in a cosmic pack.
Saturn spins tales, while Jupiter plays,
A game of tag in the nebulous bays.

Stars share their secrets, oh what a hoot,
Like twinkling jesters in a galactic suit.
I giggle along as I twirl in my chair,
An astronaut's chuckle, a bounce in the air.

Comets throw parties, they zoom and they zoom,
With meteor dancers to light up the room.
Starlit streamers cascade from above,
In this wacky expanse, it's laughter we love.

So here in the void, we chime, we cheer,
In the cosmic theater, there's nothing to fear.
With starlight as our laughter, brightening the night,
We'll dance through the cosmos, in pure delight!

## Cosmic Journeys

Out in the galaxy, stars are our pals,
They twinkle and giggle like celestial gals.
A spaceship made from kitchen supplies,
Zooming past comets, oh what a surprise!

Luis lost his sock in the Milky Way,
Now it's an orbiting laundry bouquet.
Aliens laugh as they offer a drink,
It's just cosmic coffee, or so they think!

Black holes are just portals to a new snack,
Where gravity pulls in the things we lack.
So let's take a ride on this quirky path,
With laughter and biscuits, we'll have a good laugh!

Shooting stars race with a dash of flair,
Some wear capes, others style their hair.
We'll dance with asteroids, spin like a top,
In this funny universe, we'll never stop!

**Starlight Musings**

Twinkling a greeting from lightyears away,
Stars throw a party, come join the ballet.
Galactic balloons float around with glee,
Beware of those who think they're VIP!

Wormholes are shortcuts, or so they claim,
But end up in ice cream, isn't that lame?
Asteroids might be bumpy, certainly not neat,
But they serve the best snacks, oh what a treat!

Planets wear hats that are oddly shaped,
Jupiter's crown looks like it's been draped.
Saturn's rings are just hula hoops gone rogue,
A cosmic dance-off in this starry vogue!

Cosmic comedians tell jokes out of this world,
While space whales dance, their tails unfurled.
So grab your spacesuit, let's giggle and glide,
Exploring the cosmos with laughter as our guide!

## Nebulous Thoughts

Floating through nebulae, colors abound,
Gas clouds are puff pastries, doughy and round.
Planets are brats with their own kind of flair,
They pull silly pranks like a cosmic scare!

The sun is a golden, slightly burnt toast,
It pops up each morning, a breakfast host.
Mercury's speedy, always late to the show,
While Venus just swoons, stealing the glow!

Gravity's joke? It's all about weight,
As we tumble around, let's celebrate fate.
Meteor showers raining down like confetti,
Laughing so hard, we're not even quite ready!

Glimmering orbs give the cosmos a wink,
In this vast universe, we'll always find ink.
For scribbling our tales and chuckles in flight,
Let's dance with the stars, and party all night!

## Ethereal Expressions

Celestial beings paint on the night,
With brushes of stardust, oh what a sight!
They giggle and wiggle in nebulous hues,
Chasing comets in a cosmic snooze.

UFOs zoom by with a whoosh and a cheer,
Don't mind the beeping, just "Hi, Earth, we're here!"
They swipe through galaxies, making a mess,
Claiming that light-year's just cosmic excess.

Constellations gossip like old friends, you see,
Sharing their secrets with sprinkles of glee.
Shooting stars trip over their own shining tails,
While orbiting around like joyful snails!

In the end, it's a journey of laughter and light,
Where space-time is jiggly, and everything's bright.
So join the parade with twinkling delight,
And let's dance with the cosmos, into the night!

## Cosmic Footprints

In zero gravity, I dropped my lunch,
It floated by like a hungry bunch.
My sandwich danced with stars so bright,
While I chased it down with all my might.

A comet tail waved as I sped past,
I lost my shoe - what a cosmic blast!
Asteroids chuckled, I heard them laugh,
As I tripped on a gas ball - what a gaffe!

Aliens pointed, they took a selfie,
I was the star, a galactic thrill.
With a wink, they sent me on my way,
Perhaps they'd seen my lunch delay!

In this vastness, I twirled with glee,
In cosmic chaos, I'm ever free.
I'll dine with stars, and moonbeams too,
What a meal with the universe's view!

## Interstellar Musings

As I floated past the lunar cheese,
I pondered life while tickling knees.
Asteroids roll like giant balls,
I swear they giggled as one of them falls.

My spaceship's fridge had quite the flair,
It opened wide, like it didn't care.
Out spilled snacks that defy all laws,
Chips and dips with space flavors that pause!

Met a Martian who loved to dance,
In zero G, he took a chance.
Twisting, turning, we spun in delight,
I lost my hat, it soared out of sight!

Wormholes twist like party streamers,
And I scribble notes of cosmic dreamers.
With planets as my pen and stars as ink,
Interstellar fun—what do you think?

## Celestial Constellations

The Big Dipper spilled my morning tea,
While Orion pointed and laughed at me.
I learned to juggle with Saturn's rings,
As Venus hummed and did her swing.

Stars in pajamas winked at my plight,
Navigating comets is quite a sight!
I asked for directions, they just giggled,
'Round the black hole and then we'll wiggle!'

A black hole stole my favorite sock,
I fished for it 'til I heard the clock.
Time flies out here, or so they say,
I'll find that sock another day!

With stellar sketches in my notebook bright,
I'll keep tracking cosmic joys each night.
The galaxy's a stage, my friends, take flight,
In this theater, we laugh with delight!

## A Symphony of Stardust

In the void where silence once reigned,
A melody sparked, sparks uncontained.
Each twinkling note danced through the sky,
As planets joined in with a cosmic sigh.

Shooting stars strummed on the harp of night,
While meteors drummed with all their might.
Galaxies swayed to the rhythm's beat,
As the universe grooved on cosmic feet.

I conducted asteroids with a flair,
And space whales hummed from their cool lair.
Together we played a stellar choir,
Finishing with a gleeful cosmic fire!

Thus here amid the starry dust,
We laughed, we danced, it was a must!
In this symphonic vastness, we're invited,
To jam with the cosmos, so delighted!

## The Poetry of Particles

Tiny specks dance in the dark,
A cosmic party with no remark.
They twirl around with flair and grace,
Sprinkling giggles in outer space.

Atoms whisper and tease the void,
Creating mischief, never avoid.
A neutron wiggles as it flirts,
While protons wear their polka shirts.

Planets spin, they jive and whirl,
Comets glide, giving a twirl.
With every orbit, a chuckle floats,
In this party of cosmic oats.

So grab a drink, enjoy the ride,
In this universe, absurdity's wide.
From quarks to stars, let laughter ring,
Life's a ball, let the particles sing!

## Enigmas of the Ether

In the silence between the stars,
Lies a riddle with endless czars.
Black holes giggle, hiding their charms,
While dark matter hoards all the farms.

Gravity's joke pulls us all tight,
As planets bounce in galactic light.
A nebula hiccups, spilling its dye,
While asteroids waddle, oh my, oh my!

Meteorites shoot like wild jesters,
As stardust spins in cosmic festers.
Floating through space, they crack a smile,
Hoping we catch them, if just for a while.

So ponder the quirks of this absurd place,
With each twinkling star, there's humor to trace.
Cosmic puzzles, forever in play,
Life's quite hilarious in this vast ballet!

## Whispers from the Cosmos

Listen close, there's giggles afloat,
Stars gossip lightly, krill in a boat.
Tiny quasars with secrets to share,
Spilling laughter into the stellar air.

Asteroids chuckle, their paths never straight,
Bumping and tumbling like they're on a date.
They blame the gravity for not keeping still,
While supernovas pop like popcorn at will.

Galaxies swirl, in spirals they spin,
Each new creation a cheeky grin.
Wormholes wiggle, asking us to peek,
Into dimensions where laughter's the peak.

So when you ponder the vastness so wide,
Remember the humor tucked deep inside.
Light years away, a joke just might land,
In this cosmos, together we stand!

## **Lightyears of Melancholy**

A comet trails with a frown on its face,
Longing for warmth in this cold, lonely space.
While aliens sniffle, their tears made of stars,
Sending a message wrapped up in bizarre.

Black holes sigh as they swallow their dreams,
Kicking out planets and all of their schemes.
The universe teeters on the brink of a laugh,
Yet shadows linger, like a missed photograph.

Supernovae weep, their beauty's a crime,
In a silence so loud, it echoes through time.
But even in sorrow, joy lurks near,
The stars wink at us, hiding a cheer.

So tip your hats to the cosmic parade,
For lightyears may fade, but humor won't trade.
Even in shadows, a giggle can start,
In the vastness of space, there's room for a heart!

## Starborn Stories in Celestial Patterns

In the cosmos, a twinkling spree,
Aliens giggle, drinking cosmic tea.
Asteroids dance with graceful might,
While comets throw confetti, pure delight.

Planets spin in their swirling waltz,
Mars tripped on a rock, that's not his fault!
Galaxies chuckle, collide, and play,
In this vast playground, we drift away.

Stars wear sunglasses, bright as the sun,
Chasing black holes, just for fun.
Nebulas shimmer with laughable flair,
Whispering secrets to all, everywhere.

Jupiter's moons are a wild bunch,
They hold space parties—grab a crunch!
In the fabric of night, we twinkle and trace,
These jubilant tales of our cosmic race.

## Memories Written in Light's Ephemeral Glow

Once I met a star named Fred,
In a cosmic diner, he ordered bread.
Light years traveled for a silly snack,
He said, 'I'm on a diet, can I hold back?'

Solar flares giggle, burning bright,
Their dance moves put all stars to fright.
They shook and shimmered, a vibrant sight,
While planets blushed in the soft moonlight.

There's a meteor shower, a cosmic peek,
Wishing for free tacos—what a cheek!
Astro-bunnies hop in zero-g,
Telling jokes about space, oh so free!

Stardust dreams on cosmic peaks,
Floating on laughter, that's how it speaks.
In the glow of night, let's draw our fate,
With memories that shine, don't hesitate!

## Infinite Horizons of the Celestial Song

On a comet ride, we had a blast,
Zipping past Saturn, oh what a fast!
Jupiter's storms, a twisty slide,
Each twist and turn, an interstellar ride.

Singing with stars in a cosmic jam,
Odes to black holes, oh what a slam!
Dance-offs at dawn with the Milky Way,
In the theater of space, we laugh all day.

Venus plays the ukulele, what a treat,
Plucking strings to a rhythm so sweet.
With Martian mosquitoes buzzing around,
We keep the party lively, joyfully unbound!

As beams of light form celestial chords,
We sing of adventures, without any swords.
In the vastness of night, laughter flows free,
A symphony of joy, come dance with me!

## Celestial Letters Beneath the Starlit Canopy

Under the stars, penned letters we send,
To distant worlds, where giggles extend.
Sirius writes back, 'Your jokes are a hit,'
While Draco just rolls, he can't take a sit.

Crafting our tales with meteoric zest,
Over cosmic postage, we send our best.
Puns written in stardust, a glow we embrace,
Creating a spark, in this wide, wild space.

Too many quirks, from moons that prance,
Dancing to beats in an odd tango dance.
Wishing upon satellites, laughter flows bright,
In the beauty of silence, we share our delight.

Galactic green aliens, they read with glee,
Sipping their drinks made of zero-point tea.
Beneath the starlit sky, memories ignite,
With letters of joy, we take our flight.

## Temporal Fragments Drifting Through the Cosmos

Tiny grains float in a cosmic sea,
Lost stories swirl, just like me!
Galaxies giggle, stars play hide and seek,
In this mad dance, no one's a freak.

Planets spin tales of cheese and wine,
While comets toast with a champagne shine.
Asteroids hum a merry old tune,
Sing along, folks, to the cosmic cartoon!

Black holes burp with a cheeky delight,
Sucking in the fun, oh what a sight!
Nebulas sparkle, like confetti grown,
In this universe, we're never alone.

So grab your broomstick, let's fly and frolic,
Through this zany cosmic chronicle.
With temporal fragments scattered wide,
Let's laugh together on this stellar ride.

## Interstellar Echoes of Forgotten Dreams

Whispers float by like a duck in a pond,
Echoing dreams that we all have conned.
Saturn's rings jingle with comical glee,
As space poets scribble their cosmic decree.

Aliens chuckle with their three-eyed glow,
Redefining cool with their funky show.
A meteorite wearing sunglasses too,
Zooms past and shouts, 'Hey, how do you do?'

Old dreams bounce back like a rubber ball,
Hitching rides on the sun's bright call.
While star clusters play a raucous game,
Of hide and seek, oh isn't it tame?

So let's toast to dreams in this cosmic quest,
Floating through shadows, having the best!
In a universe crazy but sweet as cream,
Let's dance in echoes of forgotten dreams.

## Aurora's Dance in the Constellation's Embrace

In a swirl of colors, the auroras prance,
Lighting up the dark in a dazzling dance.
The constellations laugh, tickled by light,
As starlit fairies twirl through the night.

Sirius winks with a mischievous grin,
While Orion trips on his belt and spins.
While galaxies twist in a jig so grand,
We'll join arms, let's make a space band!

Bright comets whizz by, like fireflies' flight,
Making wishes on trails that shimmer so bright.
Jupiter's storms giggle with delight,
This cosmic jam feels so right tonight.

So swirl with the colors, embrace the sky,
Tickling stars while we laugh and cry.
In this grand ballet, let's take our place,
Together in wonder, in the cosmic space.

## Whispers from the Eclipsed Moon

In the shadows of twilight, secrets awake,
The moon chuckles softly, for goodness' sake!
Jokes from the shadows, a wink and a nudge,
Even craters have stories, all of them grudge.

Hidden behind clouds in a sneaky disguise,
The moon's giggling fits light up the skies.
Stars point and wonder, 'What's with the fuss?'
Eclipses in laughter, causing a fuss.

Even comets stop for a brief little chat,
While constellations ponder, "What's up with that?"
Shooting stars crack jokes, with wishes in tow,
Floating through darkness, putting on a show.

So let's listen closely to the moon's merry tune,
Whispers and giggles, from dusk until noon.
Through shadows and light, we all find our way,
In the laughter of space, come join the play!

## Celestial Whispers Among the Stars

In a galaxy vast, a cheeky star laughed,
Shooting across the night, making light of the past.
"Why do comets cry?" it winked with glee,
"Because they miss their tails, just wait and see!"

Planets spin round in a dizzying dance,
While asteroids play hide-and-seek at a glance.
"Catch me if you can!" they shout with delight,
"Oh, come join the fun! It's a cosmic night!"

Nebulas swirl in fantastic displays,
Talking in colors, in whimsical ways.
"Look at me, I'm pink!" one declared with pride,
"But purple's my favorite when I spin and glide!"

Jupiter chuckled, tickled by moons,
While Saturn's rings played syncopated tunes.
Together they laughed, in a joyous parade,
For in the night sky, there's no room for shade.

## Galactic Reverie in Starlit Dreams

Splitting the night like a cosmic pie,
Stars whisper secrets as they twinkle by.
"Did you hear about Venus?" the Orion spoke,
"She tried to host parties, but the sun just woke!"

Cosmic giggles rang in a meteor shower,
As stars gathered round, with delicious star power.
"Who brought the snacks?" a tiny one cried,
"Oh please, not more stardust, I've had enough fried!"

Satellites shared tales of their trips far and wide,
"We saw a black hole! It was quite a ride!"
They laughed at the chaos of their orbits so wild,
As they zoomed past the sun, like a hyperactive child.

In this galactic realm, there's never a frown,
With humor galore spinning round and round.
So relish the laughter that light-years ignite,
And dream with the stars on this magical night.

## Cosmic Chronicles of Forgotten Comets

Comets long lost tell tales in the dark,
Once they were famous, now they've lost their spark.
"Remember my tail?" one whimpered in fright,
"Now I'm just a dot, what a fall from height!"

They gather together for a reunion spree,
Gossiping warmly, sipping cosmic tea.
"Last I heard Halley was hitting the road,
But now he's just parked—what a heavy load!"

"I was once a sight, and I caused a commotion,
Now I'm just a relic drifting through the ocean!"
They chuckle together as they float and glide,
Recalling the moments of their celestial pride.

But despite how they feel, with their tails in retreat,
They dance through the void—still a charming feat.
For in their own way, they sparkle in flight,
A reminder of glory, lost in the night.

## Stardust Serenade in the Void

Under the cover of a twinkling dome,
Stars croon and hum as they drift far from home.
"Oh, look at that dwarf!" giggled one bright flare,
"He forgot his lines in the galactic faire!"

A meteorite tumbled, declaring a show,
"Catch me if you can! But I'll probably go slow!"
The audience gasped as it spun in a twist,
"You call that a comet? Just look at your list!"

Planets predicted a raucous good time,
Swapping their roles, they danced on a dime.
"I'll be the sun with a wig made of rings!
And you, little asteroid, just stick to your flings!"

So laugh with the cosmos and whirl in delight,
For silliness sparkles in the blanket of night.
With every bright twinkle, may joy reappear,
In this vast universe, let laughter be clear!

## Breaths in the Expanse

In the void where wild things glide,
A comet sneezed, and stars did hide.
Asteroids laugh, they bounce and roll,
While aliens dance, they lose control.

Gravity gives a playful tug,
As planets enjoy a cozy hug.
Moonbeams giggle, light as air,
While stars trade jokes without a care.

A supernova's flash brings cheer,
As black holes whisper, 'Not quite here.'
Nebulas swirl like a twirling dress,
Cosmic chaos, who'd ever guess?

Lost in laughter, we float around,
In this vast world where fun is found.
So come take flight, embrace the jest,
In the universe, we're all blessed!

## Astral Anecdotes

Once a star tried to wear a tie,
But slipped and fell, oh my, oh my!
Galaxies giggled in swirling bliss,
At the sight of that stellar miss.

Planets play tag, and meteors zoom,
While robots dance in metallic gloom.
Solar flares join in the fun,
With a bright eruption—just a pun!

A space whale sings a cosmic tune,
While comets wish upon the moon.
Quasars wink with a twinkling glee,
What a wild hug in this artistry!

Lost in the midst of celestial cheer,
Stars enact stories we all can hear.
So grab your ship, let's take a ride,
Through the funny side of the cosmic tide!

## Celestial Remembrances

In the skies where laughter swells,
A rogue planet hides, and oh, it tells.
"Why do stars shine while comets dart?
Because I'm too heavy, that's my part!"

A quirky quasar beams a grin,
As galaxies swirl, they spin and spin.
Asteroids gossip as they collide,
Forming new tales of the celestial ride.

The sun spilled juice on the Milky Way,
The cosmic party lasted all day.
Martians play poker on little green rocks,
While Saturn spins with its breezy frocks.

Jupiter's storm joins in the song,
While stardust floats, it won't be long.
A cosmic laugh that cracks the night,
In this boundless dance of pure delight!

## Constellation Chronicles

Once Orion chased a shooting star,
But tripped on his belt, oh how bizarre!
The Bear and the Lion roared with glee,
As they watched their friend tumble free.

Pleiades twinkled, wearing bright hats,
While nearby, a planet danced with cats.
Oh, what follies among the stars,
With light-years echoing the best bizarre!

Nebulae giggle and spin in delight,
While comets race, chasing the night.
Saturn spins tales in its ringed embrace,
Of how he lost his fuzzy face!

So gather 'round, and share some cheer,
In the tapestry of cosmos near.
Where laughter twinkles in cosmic folds,
In tales of the universe yet untold!

www.ingramcontent.com/pod-product-compliance
Lightning Source LLC
Chambersburg PA
CBHW071816160426
43209CB00003B/106